Rethinking Civilian Stabilization and Reconstruction

AUTHORS
Robert D. Lamb
Kathryn Mixon
Joy Aoun

A Report of the CSIS Program on Crisis, Conflict, and Cooperation

November 2013

50 YEARS | CHARTING OUR FUTURE

CSIS | CENTER FOR STRATEGIC & INTERNATIONAL STUDIES

ROWMAN & LITTLEFIELD
Lanham • Boulder • New York • Toronto • Plymouth, UK

AECOM IRD

About CSIS—50th Anniversary Year

For 50 years, the Center for Strategic and International Studies (CSIS) has developed solutions to the world's greatest policy challenges. As we celebrate this milestone, CSIS scholars are developing strategic insights and bipartisan policy solutions to help decisionmakers chart a course toward a better world.

CSIS is a nonprofit organization headquartered in Washington, D.C. The Center's 220 full-time staff and large network of affiliated scholars conduct research and analysis and develop policy initiatives that look into the future and anticipate change.

Founded at the height of the Cold War by David M. Abshire and Admiral Arleigh Burke, CSIS was dedicated to finding ways to sustain American prominence and prosperity as a force for good in the world. Since 1962, CSIS has become one of the world's preeminent international institutions focused on defense and security; regional stability; and transnational challenges ranging from energy and climate to global health and economic integration.

Former U.S. senator Sam Nunn has chaired the CSIS Board of Trustees since 1999. Former deputy secretary of defense John J. Hamre became the Center's president and chief executive officer in April 2000.

CSIS does not take specific policy positions; accordingly, all views expressed herein should be understood to be solely those of the author(s).

ISBN: 978-1-4422-2779-8 (pb); 978-1-4422-2780-4 (eBook)

Center for Strategic & International Studies
1616 Rhode Island Avenue, NW
Washington, DC 20036
202-887-0200 | www.csis.org

Rowman & Littlefield
4501 Forbes Boulevard
Lanham, MD 20706
301-459-3366 | www.rowman.com

Contents

Preface

Civilian stabilization and reconstruction is not a field with small ambitions. When political leaders want to respond to foreign crises but do not want to use military power, they send diplomats, aid workers, advisers, researchers, logisticians, planners, and other civilians with needed skills to the edges and sometimes into the middle of war zones—or refugee camps, foreign capitals, provincial towns, or isolated villages. There, they try to figure out what it will take to protect communities or minorities, persuade combatants to cease fire, prevent further attacks, evacuate those in danger, negotiate peace, or help people recover from the trauma and destruction of conflict. The scale of the challenge is usually far beyond the capacity of a few overtaxed outsiders to even understand, much less resolve; even knowing which locals to ask for or offer help is fraught with risk, the potential to exacerbate political or sectarian tensions, for example. It is not easy work—clear successes are too few to be professionally rewarding (though frequent enough to be worth pursuing)—but it is necessary work.

Over the past few years, CSIS's Program on Crisis, Conflict, and Cooperation (C3), which I direct, has been taking a step back, after many years of working on Afghanistan, Pakistan, and (earlier) Iraq, to ask some basic questions about the state and future of the field. The findings of our research—and that of many other excellent scholars worldwide—has convinced me that it is time for a pretty fundamental rethinking about what this field is and what it should be. Our work has focused mainly on American capabilities and institutions but is broadly relevant to non-U.S. institutions involved in this work worldwide.

- **There will always be pressure to intervene in foreign crises.** A new protest movement, coup, conflict, or war begins somewhere in the world, on average, about every three weeks, according to the CSIS Potential Transitions Dataset, and U.S. leaders are almost always under pressure to do something in response. Most foreign crises begin and end without any significant involvement by the United States, which resists the pressure to intervene about three or four times more often than it actually intervenes. That still means, however, that about once every two months, on average, the United States does try to materially influence the outcome of a foreign crisis by diplomacy, aid, or force. That level of demand for U.S. intervention capabilities is not likely to diminish any time in the near future, despite public fatigue after long wars in Afghanistan and Iraq.[1] The events taking place in Egypt, Turkey, and Syria in the

1. Robert D. Lamb and Sadika Hameed, with Joy Aoun, Kevin Jones, Kathryn Mixon, and Adam Parker, *U.S. Policy Responses to Potential Transitions: A New Dataset of Political Protests, Conflicts, and Coups* (Washington, D.C.: CSIS, March 2013).

weeks leading up to the July 2013 CSIS conference on civilian stabilization and reconstruction amply demonstrated this point.

- **Most U.S. interventions use civilian power.** Although the United States does not necessarily aid all political transitions and potential transitions, it has a clear preference for using civilian capabilities—diplomacy and aid—in those situations it does get involved in. Less than a third of U.S. interventions involve military capabilities; most are civilian interventions. Even when military power is brought to bear, it is almost always as a last resort. In other words, U.S. leaders, regardless of political party, clearly prefer to respond to crises and political transitions using civilian rather than military capabilities.[2]

- **The demand for civilian power exceeds the supply.** Despite this clear preference for civilian-led responses, U.S. military capabilities are "more readily available, more strategically postured, and certainly better resourced" than its civilian tools. "The agonizing debates about whether and how to respond to foreign crises often seem to center on how to avoid involving the U.S. military. That job would be far easier if a more robust set of civilian tools was available."[3] Clearly, the United States needs a better set of nonmilitary options for responding to internal conflicts and political transitions.

- **Civilian agencies do not have the support needed to meet the demand.** In 2012 the C3 program at CSIS hosted series of workshops during its tenth anniversary to review the state of the field.[4] It found that "U.S. government officials and the American public in general have difficulty accepting the inevitability of U.S. involvement in . . . efforts to stabilize countries affected by conflict and to help them recover afterwards." Further, "government officials, Congress, and the American public do not acknowledge that the civilian expertise and resources needed to do this work is inadequate relative to the demand."[5] It concluded that "the case has not been made to the American public that most U.S. efforts going forward are unlikely to follow the Afghanistan and Iraq model. Nor has the case been successfully made that the demand for this kind of work is not likely to subside, although the complexity of addressing instability in the future will challenge U.S. military and civilian capacities."[6] One consequence of the failure to make this case successfully is the failure to attract adequate support for the changes that civilian agencies need in order to operate more effectively in conflict and post-conflict environments.

---

2. Ibid.

3. Robert D. Lamb, preface to *U.S. Policy Responses to Potential Transitions*, iv.

4. C3 was founded in 2002 as the Post-Conflict Reconstruction Project. The PCR Project, as it was known, inherited its mandate from the Post-Conflict Reconstruction Commission, which had been launched jointly by CSIS and the Association of the U.S. Army in 2001. The PCR Project was renamed in 2011 to better reflect its research portfolio.

5. Robert D. Lamb, Johanna Mendelson Forman, and Liora Danan, *Inevitable Conflicts, Avoidable Failures: Preparing for the Third Generation of Conflict, Stabilization, and Reconstruction Operations* (Washington, D.C.: CSIS, July 2012), 1.

6. Ibid., 7.

- **Civilian agencies do not have the capacity to meet the demand.** C3's recent research on problems of aid absorption in developing countries found that a major constraint on absorptive capacity, aside from technical capacity in the recipient communities, was "donor delivery capacity," that is, the ability of donor organizations to learn and apply lessons, select feasible aid objectives, customize aid to local conditions, and deliver on promises.[7] C3's tenth anniversary workshops found that many development, stabilization, reconstruction, political transition, and other professionals believe that such weaknesses are due not only to the lack of public and official support for what they do but also to their own organizations' failures to institutionalize the lessons of the past.[8] Many have their own hypotheses about why lessons and evidence are not always institutionalized, including ignorance, politics, bureaucracy, and ideology. Given the complexity of the donor environment, however, it is likely that no single explanation is sufficient. C3 has identified 24 potential explanations in six organizational functions (leadership, personnel, budgeting, security, contracting, planning) across four dimensions (knowledge, processes, culture, and incentives).[9] But not enough research has been done on donor organizations themselves to shed more light on the constraints to delivery capacity.

While our program continues to pursue research on all these issues, we wanted to bring some key officials and experts together in Washington to begin a public conversation about the capabilities and support this field needs. To that end, in July 2013 we hosted a daylong conference, Rethinking Civilian Stabilization and Reconstruction, and invited more than 20 speakers and more than 200 professionals to think about what lessons have been learned—and what is stopping us from learning those that have not been learned. As I said in my opening remarks at the conference:

> Conflicts aren't going away. We are going to be getting involved in [them] for many years, over and over again. . . . So today as you listen to all the speakers, as you raise questions, as you talk with each other over coffee, I want you to think closely about the two basic messages of the conference today: . . . the American people can't lose faith in this field because [given how frequently we are called on] the truth is the demand for this field isn't going away. And we in this field need to be worthy of their faith by continuing to rethink how we operate, what we're trying to accomplish, and how we're studying it.[10]

We did not come up with definitive answers, but I think we succeeded in planting the seeds of a new research agenda focused far more squarely on how our own organizations

7. Robert D. Lamb and Kathryn Mixon, *Rethinking Absorptive Capacity: A New Framework, Applied to Afghanistan's Police Training Program* (Washington, D.C.: CSIS, June 2013); Robert D. Lamb, Kathryn Mixon, and Andrew Halterman, *Absorptive Capacity in the Security and Justice Sectors: Assessing Obstacles to Success in the Donor-Recipient Relationship* (Washington, D.C.: CSIS, June 2013).

8. Lamb, Mendelson Forman, and Danan, *Inevitable Conflicts, Avoidable Failures.*

9. Robert D. Lamb, "Measuring Absorptive Capacity: A New Framework for Estimating Constraints," CSIS policy brief, May 2013, 7–8.

10. Robert D. Lamb, remarks at *Rethinking Civilian Stabilization and Reconstruction*, CSIS conference, July 16, 2013, Washington, D.C.

operate, and how they need to change, to develop the capabilities and attract the public support needed to bring peace when asked or accomplish critical foreign policy objectives when called upon.

This conference would not have been possible without the generous financial support of International Relief and Development (IRD) and AECOM. The authors are particularly grateful to Arthur Keys and Jeffrey Grieco of IRD, and to John Dionisio and David Wall of AECOM.

The intellectual content of the conference was shaped by its speakers, panelists, and moderators. A full conference agenda and speaker biographies are appended to this report, but the authors would like to thank all of them here: Liliana Ayalde, Frederick Barton, John Blaney, William Deng Deng, James Dobbins, Juan Pablo Franco Jiménez, François Grignon, Husain Haqqani, John Hamre, David Ignatius, Robert Jenkins, Arthur Keys, James Kunder, Jason Matus, Sean McFate, Johanna Mendelson Forman, Franklin Moore, Andrew Natsios, Jonathan Temin, David Wall, and Rubén Zamora. It seems likely that not all of these speakers and panelists would agree with everything in this report, and nothing here should be attributed to any of them. I take full responsibility for its content. I would also like to thank my coauthors, Kathryn Mixon and Joy Aoun, for organizing the conference and capturing its insights, and research intern Hannah K. Brown for editorial support to this report.

—Robert D. Lamb
September 15, 2013
Washington, D.C.

Rethinking Civilian Stabilization and Reconstruction

On July 16, 2013, more than 200 policymakers and experts attended what for most of the day was a standing-room-only conference at the Center for Strategic and International Studies (CSIS) in Washington, D.C. The participants—drawn from government, nongovernmental organizations (NGOs), the private sector, and the media—all were professionally engaged in some aspect of peace, conflict, stabilization, reconstruction, humanitarian response, or political transition work. Over eight hours, they listened to 22 experts and practitioners discuss the significant role the United States plays in such efforts worldwide. Can the United States prevent or end conflicts and protect its interests without using its military? Do U.S. civilian institutions have the right mix of support, funding, and capabilities to respond to major crises and political transitions? What do those institutions do well? What needs improvement? Where is more support for civilian capabilities needed? And what should practitioners and researchers do to help the United States institutionalize the right lessons from history and on-the-ground experience?

This conference was motivated by recent research from CSIS's Program on Crisis, Conflict, and Cooperation (C3). Over the past two years, C3's research program has found that the pressure for the United States to intervene in foreign crises has long existed and is not likely to subside in the foreseeable future; most U.S. interventions are civilian interventions, while military interventions are relatively rare and almost always a last resort; the demand for civilian power exceeds its supply when it comes to finding ways to respond to foreign crises without resorting to military force; the civilian agencies that have the needed capabilities do not have the needed institutional or financial support; and as a consequence, civilian agencies do not have enough capacity to prevent, deescalate, resolve, or mitigate the effects of conflicts, compared to what U.S. leaders clearly wish they were able to accomplish.[1]

In sum, the demand for civilian capabilities—diplomacy and aid in the subdisciplines of conflict prevention and management, peace building, stabilization, reconstruction, consolidation, transition, and so on—remains high and unmet.

1. See Robert D. Lamb and Sadika Hameed, with Joy Aoun, Kevin Jones, Kathryn Mixon, and Adam Parker, *U.S. Policy Responses to Potential Transitions: A New Dataset of Political Protests, Conflicts, and Coups* (Washington, D.C.: CSIS, March 2013); Lamb, Mendelson Forman, and Danan, *Inevitable Conflicts, Avoidable Failures*, 1; Lamb and Mixon, *Rethinking Absorptive Capacity*; and Robert D. Lamb, Kathryn Mixon, and Andrew Halterman, *Absorptive Capacity in the Security and Justice Sectors: Assessing Obstacles to Success in the Donor-Recipient Relationship* (Washington, D.C.: CSIS, June 2013); all are available at http://csis.org/program/c3.

This research has two important implications. First, the United States as a society needs to learn how to support the civilian institutions and capabilities that are required to do this work. Second, the organizations and individuals involved in this work need to learn how to institutionalize the lessons of history and experience. These two needs are related: without adequate support, the field cannot improve, and if the field does not improve, it will not attract support. The main purpose of the Rethinking Civilian Stabilization and Reconstruction conference at CSIS was to convene leading scholars and practitioners to start finding ways to turn that vicious cycle into a virtuous cycle: support improves competence, which attracts support.

The imperative to attract public support for this field is not meant to encourage more U.S. interventions in foreign crises. On the contrary, C3's own data analysis found that U.S. interventions do not reliably lead to outcomes that are favorable either to U.S. interests or to the interests and well-being of people involved in or affected by conflicts (a finding that recommends caution and modesty in intervention decisions).[2] This point was made explicit at the start of the conference: the demand for better crisis-response tools "doesn't mean the United States should be intervening everywhere in the world. It does mean that there is always going to pressure for the United States to do so, and there is always going to be the temptation for the United States to do so—which means that once in a while the United States is going to intervene somehow."[3]

Rather than encouraging foreign adventurism, the point of the conference was to find ways to improve the nonmilitary options the United States has to reduce violence, prevent or deescalate armed conflicts, mitigate their effects, and help people recover from them. Having robust capabilities such as these could reduce the need to use military capabilities—using force can put lives, funds, and relationships at greater risk—once conflicts spiral out of control.

Speakers and attendees alike were therefore encouraged both to reflect upon what lessons have and have not been learned and, more importantly, to start thinking more pointedly about what is preventing their own organizations from institutionalizing lessons that have been known, but not consistently applied, for decades.

This report presents the results of those discussions, summarizing the key points from each session in the conference. Two of those sessions focused on several concrete cases of U.S. assistance to countries emerging from conflict: Colombia and Liberia in one session and South Sudan in the other. The intention of these panel discussions was to give officials who had been directly involved in these programs the opportunity to provide an insider's view of the successes and challenges they faced on the ground and hear what concrete lessons they extracted from the experience. Other sessions featured individuals with many years of experience in making, implementing, or studying policy in a wide variety of

---

2. Lamb and Hameed, *U.S. Policy Responses to Potential Transitions*, vii.
3. Robert D. Lamb, remarks at *Rethinking Civilian Stabilization and Reconstruction*, CSIS conference, July 16, 2013, Washington, D.C.

conflict environments, each offering their own much broader perspectives of the challenges the field faces. The lunchtime session featured foreign officials who have been on the receiving end of U.S. assistance to their countries, sharing their views about what the United States does well and what it does poorly. The concluding section of this report highlights some of the most important themes that emerged from these discussions and some thoughts on the future of the stabilization and reconstruction field, including areas that require focused research or more attention from policymakers.

Are Americans Losing Faith in Civilian Power?

The conference opened with some of the themes introduced at the start of this report. At a time when the American public and most policymakers are tired of the time, lives, and resources that have been spent rebuilding foreign countries, the world is experiencing a new wave of political instability and conflict in the Middle East and North Africa, not to mention new offensive peacekeeping operations in Africa, growing concern over violence in Central America, and significant political transitions in Myanmar/Burma and South Sudan. It is tempting to say that the need for civilian capabilities to meet these challenges has never been higher, but in fact the need has been high for decades—it just has not been fully met. Most U.S. officials do not want to deploy military forces for these contingencies. This might therefore be a good time for the United States to rethink its civilian capabilities—both to support them and to improve them.

It is in the interest of the organizations and individuals involved in peace, conflict, stabilization, reconstruction, and transition efforts to do a better job educating the American public and U.S. policymakers, especially in Congress, about what they do, why they do it, and what their efforts have accomplished. Accomplishments have included protecting U.S. interests by contributing to stability, promoting humanitarian values by shaping reconstruction, or saving money by preventing conflicts that would otherwise demand much more expensive responses. They also have to do a better job explaining that progress can be made with enough time and resources, but that the situations they are asked to assist are complex—often not only locally but geopolitically as well—and they are not amenable to simple or quick solutions, as is too often demanded by elected officials, media personalities, and activists. Real progress has been made in interagency coordination; there is certainly a long way to go, but the State Department, the U.S. Agency for International Development (USAID), and the Defense Department understand each other better and work together far more today than they did 10 years ago. There have been successes in places such as the Balkans and Colombia; even Afghanistan has made substantial progress in development and governance compared to how the Taliban regime left it more than a decade ago. If nothing else, there is a large cadre of American civilians who today have a great deal of experience working in conflict zones, or what sometimes are called "contingency environments," and who therefore know the distinct challenges they pose as compared to more stable development environments.

But telling the American public that its civilian institutions are capable of doing this sort of work might not ring true to anyone paying close attention to the news, as U.S.

leaders repeatedly seek ways to avoid using military power in response to escalating crises in places such as Egypt and Syria. When it comes to making a strategic difference in complex crisis situations, civilian power really is quite limited. There are good reasons for that but there is a strong belief within and outside of this field that those limitations cannot be explained simply by referring to the complexity of the situations and the competing interests and values involved in trying to resolve them.

Claims about this field's relevance and capabilities would ring much more true, some pointed out, if they were more often accompanied by a hard look at the field's self-imposed limitations, such as failures to deliver on promises, form constructive relationships with local populations, include marginalized groups, coordinate efforts, or measure progress toward tangible outcomes. Those who do this work have learned some things from history and experience, but significant gaps in institutionalizing this learning remain. To take a few examples cited at the opening of the conference:

- In 1928 an economist named Allyn Young published an article in which he observed that even an industrial dictator, with all the power he needed to move capital and labor, could not condense half a century's worth of normal economic progress into just a few years.[4] Yet today, 85 years later, development strategies and "road maps" designed for countries affected by conflict habitually demand equality, the rule of law, compliance with human rights norms, an end to corruption, and reintegration of former combatants into society, all within four or five years. These are important and laudable ambitions, but they are the work of generations, as European and North American societies themselves have experienced. Overpromising fast progress in countries emerging from conflict can raise expectations beyond what is constructive.
- In 1949 the World Bank published its fourth annual report, in which it presented some lessons from its first years: development and reconstruction in any society should be led by the people who live in that society; any assistance outsiders want to give can play at best a supporting role; donors should coordinate with each other to avoid overwhelming local institutions; projects should be customized to local needs and conditions, not blindly copied from what has worked in other contexts; and some of the most important impediments to progress in development have to do with donors' knowledge, expectations, assumptions, and ambitions and not simply with the capacity of recipients to absorb or implement foreign assistance.[5] Any reader even remotely familiar with the practices and controversies of this field will recognize that these problems continue to vex donors 64 years later.
- In 1965 Albert O. Hirschman argued that what development professionals consider local obstacles to development sometimes turn out not to be obstacles after all. What

---

4. Allyn A. Young, "Increasing Returns and Economic Progress," *The Economic Journal* 38, no. 152 (December 1928): 534. This article and the works cited in the following two footnotes are discussed further in the literature review of Lamb and Mixon, *Rethinking Absorptive Capacity*, 4–22.

5. International Bank for Reconstruction and Development, *Fourth Annual Report to the Board of Governors, 1948–1949* (Washington: IBRD, 1949), 8.

outsiders think might work in a place might not be what locals think can work, because the human capacity for survival and improvisation is a lot larger that outsiders sometimes recognize.[6] Yet 48 years later, development and reconstruction projects are more often treated like engineering challenges than field experiments; perversely, improvisation is sometimes actively discouraged by the incentives donor organizations place on program managers to hold them accountable for results. Improvising, experimenting, and taking risks in the field are not generally the best ways to advance one's career.

Arguing that success in these environments requires time and resources or favorable geopolitical and local conditions is true but incomplete. U.S. leaders need civilian power to be able to make strategic differences in the short term, to avoid the resort to military force. And, as Arthur Keys observed in his opening remarks, vulnerable populations cannot wait for ideal conditions to fall into place before effective development comes along. It is important to bring civilians in as early as possible in the development process, and therefore important to be sure they have the knowledge, skills, and support they need to make a real difference.

Stabilization and Reconstruction beyond Afghanistan

Participants and speakers had mixed feelings about Afghanistan. On the one hand, they are well aware that the overall effort is viewed by many as a failure, because the Taliban continue to control territory, the government's effectiveness has not met expectations, corruption remains rampant, and the security forces do not yet have the capacity to operate independently. Judged against the ambitions set in the country's constitution and various international declarations, the civilian effort cannot be judged a success.

On the other hand, considering the extremely low levels of government effectiveness and human development Afghans suffered under the Taliban, it is hard to argue that significant progress has not been made. Economic growth and human development have improved at a higher rate than in other post-conflict countries. There is a functioning government and economy; although both hardly meet the needs of most Afghans, they do so relatively more effectively than they did 12 years ago. There are functioning security forces, even if they have not yet reached a level of capability and professionalism that will enable them to operate independently for many years. And there is an active civil society, even if its members are not as effective, representative, or safe as many of their counterparts around the world. For all the talk of international military forces withdrawing to much lower levels in 2014, nobody seems to expect the civilian assistance programs will completely disappear. International support to reconstruction and peace building will likely decline but it will continue for many years. And given the sheer number of civilians

6. Albert O. Hirschman, "Obstacles to Development: A Classification and a Quasi-Vanishing Act," *Economic Development and Cultural Change* 13, no. 4 (July 1965): 391.

who now have experience doing development, stabilization, reconstruction, and related work in war zones—both Afghanistan and Iraq—there are today probably more people qualified for this field than at any time in recent memory.

Yet instead of all of that expertise and experience—the failures and the successes alike—being consolidated into a set of lessons and institutions with the capacity to do this work more effectively, reconstruction fatigue looks to be leading to a retrenchment, which risks the loss of a capability that is certain to be in demand in other contingencies for many years to come.

Finding a way to institutionalize this capability is going to be a challenge in this environment, even apart from declining public attention and support. USAID depends too much on contracting and its bureaucracy worries too much about what Congress thinks. The U.S. Institute of Peace is hesitant to allow itself to be used as an instrument of national power. The Bureau for Conflict and Stabilization Operations at the State Department is too small relative to its mission. The Central Intelligence Agency (CIA) seems to be returning to its more traditional role in intelligence. Nongovernmental organizations are not always well positioned to contribute to reconstruction in their own countries when the political climate is unfavorable. And the U.S. military seems to be shifting away from building capacity for counterinsurgency and stabilization operations, which included capabilities traditionally undertaken by civilians, in favor of more conventional operations.

In many crisis situations, there are usually very good geopolitical reasons and very good local reasons outsiders including the United States have difficulty acting without constraint, as James Dobbins suggested. Using too much power—civilian or military—in response to such crises could threaten other vital interests in its relations with other countries (needlessly antagonizing Russia or China, for example, or inadvertently strengthening Iran). And understanding local conditions—including identifying reliable partners—is extremely difficult in complex conflicts where multiple groups regularly form and break alliances and change their publicly stated reasons for fighting.

Yet despite those constraints—or perhaps because of them—learning how to use civilian power effectively in crisis situations is imperative. As David Ignatius argued, "The agenda couldn't be larger and the stakes couldn't be higher . . . What you in this room do is at the center of our national security going forward."

U.S. Support to Transitions in Colombia and Liberia

It is common in this field to distinguish between "normal" development work and development work carried out in places experiencing or recovering from conflict and violence. What might be possible to achieve in places without significant conflict or violence is not always possible to achieve in less stable environments. The difference between development and stabilization, however, is not always appreciated by the media, the public, and policymakers. As one consequence, for example, those who carry out stabilization and related efforts are often required to follow many of the same legal requirements that regulate normal development, even though this reduces the flexibility that is needed in contingency environments. Without a broader understanding of the differences between development and stabilization efforts, the latter are likely to continue being constrained in ways that limit their effectiveness. The conference's morning panel was convened to educate policymakers and the public about these differences and to discuss the special challenges of stabilization. Colombia and Liberia were chosen as the cases to be discussed because they represented relatively successful stabilization efforts and therefore could demonstrate the limits to what might be possible under current authorities and practices.

In Colombia, where areas formerly controlled by guerrillas were under the government's control for the first time in decades, U.S. support helped the Colombian government consolidate its control. In the short term security was established and the foundations for longer-term improvements in economic growth and social capital were put in place. The United States minimized its public role, enabling Colombian institutions to take the lead and the credit for local consolidation efforts. Implementing partners took risks that paid off and local leadership emerged in ways that helped the community find new ways to solve collective problems. While multiple U.S. and Colombian agencies worked together well on the stabilization effort, planning for the handoff to normal development institutions started too late and some momentum was lost when the U.S. transition programming ended.

In Liberia, once a cease-fire was in place, U.S. support helped the military make the transition from international to local control. Politics complicated the effort, but the removal of Charles Taylor from Liberia simplified the politics and made it possible to move forward on the remaining efforts. Implementation was not linear because a wide variety of issues kept arising, forcing those on the ground to improvise—it was not possible to move forward step by step—and in general they had the flexibility they needed to do so. It helped that the United States worked reasonably well with other international partners, creating a "web of peace" that helped maintain the momentum of the peace process and prevent backsliding into conflict when complications arose. As former combatants were demobilized, finding them jobs contributed to their not returning to combat. As new soldiers were recruited, they were trained, but while the training was paid for by the international community, the finance ministry's capacity to pay them after training was completed did not keep up with demand.

Even in successful stabilization programs, there will not be an identifiable moment when stabilization ends and development begins. The activities sometimes look similar, but their objectives differ and the organizations involved in them differ. That means the stabilization institutions and development institutions need to work together early on to ensure a smooth transition from one to another over time. Both need to work with security, justice, and humanitarian institutions to ensure the broader context of their work is proceeding in a mutually reinforcing way. Immediate results are needed to create and maintain momentum, but plans are needed to link short-term efforts with longer-term development.

Local conditions differ radically from one situation to the next, and any given situation can change very quickly. Policymakers and implementers, therefore, need to be flexible and adaptive to get those situations to the point where normal development institutions can take over. The need for immediate results does not always leave time for program managers to understand enough about local conditions to prepare detailed plans, however. At least some early efforts will need to be treated like experiments, in which failed efforts are abandoned and lessons are channeled into innovative efforts. What most places experiencing instability have in common is the difficulty of effecting large-scale changes quickly. It is imperative, therefore, that the objectives for stabilization and reconstruction efforts should not be overly ambitious. Even more important, the efforts need to be led by locals: outsiders are a catalyst, not a substitute, for local action. In short, flexibility and local leadership are needed because there is no recipe for how to succeed in stabilization for any particular place.

Working with Donors: Views from Recipient-Country Officials

In 2002 a high-level forum of donors meeting in Rome outlined some principles for aid effectiveness. Principles included respect for recipient countries' priorities and leadership and commitments to improve cooperation and flexibility. At a similar forum in Paris in 2005, donors and recipients committed themselves to making progress toward improving recipient-country ownership, donor alignment with local systems and priorities, donor harmonization of procedures and programs, a focus on results rather than activities, and mutual accountability between donors and recipients. A third high-level forum took place in Accra, Ghana, in 2008 to develop an agenda for action toward achieving those goals. The fourth forum in Busan, South Korea, in 2011—preceded by a study that found donors were not fulfilling their earlier commitments—established a partnership intended to institutionalize those commitments. Other international fora and donor reports over the past decade have produced similar declarations about the importance of country ownership, donor coordination, sensitivity to local conditions, and other such principles.[7]

7. See, for example, "A New Deal for Engagement in Fragile States," International Dialogue on Peacebuilding and Statebuilding (December 2011), http://www.oecd.org/dataoecd/35/50/49151944.pdf; "Paris Declaration on Aid Effectiveness: Ownership, Harmonization, Alignment, Results, and Mutual Accountability," Organization for Economic Cooperation and Development (March 2005), http://www.oecd.org/dataoecd/15/3/46874580.pdf; "Accra Agenda for Action," Organization for Economic Cooperation and Development (September 2008), http://www.oecd.org/dataoecd/58/16/41202012.pdf; "Bogota Statement: Towards Effective and Inclusive Development Partnerships," Steering Committee of the Bogota High Level Event on South-South Cooperation and Capacity Development (March 2010), http://www.aideffectiveness.org/busanhlf4/images/stories/hlf4/Bogota_Statement_FINAL.pdf; "Dili Declaration: A New Vision for Peacebuilding and Statebuilding," International Dialogue on Peacebuilding and Statebuilding (April 2010), http://www.aideffectiveness.org/ busanhlf4/images/stories/hlf4/Dili_Declaration.pdf; "Towards a Comprehensive Paradigm for Decent Work and Development

The foreign officials who spoke on the July 2013 CSIS conference's lunchtime panel—all had significant experience working with donors on stabilization and transition efforts in their respective countries (South Sudan, El Salvador, and Pakistan)—spoke passionately about these same issues. They did so in a way that made it clear that, while the donors' support to their countries is greatly appreciated, the form it takes is too often inconsistent with the donors' own declarations and repeated commitments. Country ownership and respect, for example, were cited repeatedly as things officials in recipient countries feel are often missing in the donor-recipient relationship. "Recipients don't 'own'—they are 'told,'" said Rubén Zamora of El Salvador, in comments echoed by the other panelists. "They don't have a voice. To try to produce change with stability, you have to have a voice to do it."[8]

Recipients, in other words, are often the "forgotten partners" in the search for solutions. Recipient officials and communities usually already have innovative ideas, just not the resources to implement them. But while it is constructive when donors and recipients share their ideas and listen to each other, in the end it is the donors who will fund ideas they like and not fund ideas they do not like. In the speakers' experience, projects designed and managed by locals familiar with the community tend to be more successful than those with project managers who are not from the area. Some local organizations, however, get repeat funding not necessarily because they are good at identifying local concerns and overcoming local constraints but often because they do a good job implementing projects the donors want, regardless of whether it is what the community wants or needs. Unless more voices in the recipient communities and countries are heard, the speakers argued, the aid provided is likely to be wasted or cause needless disruptions.

The panelists were passionate in arguing that donor-driven solutions to stabilization problems are less likely to work than community-driven solutions or real partnerships. Donors tend to be more ambitious and complicated than they need to be. "How many studies do you need to figure out how to run a school?" asked Husain Haqqani of Pakistan. "It should be simple: go to the community and ask them, 'What do you need?'"[9] Donors also tend to overlearn lessons from successful efforts and use favored approaches as blueprints. William Deng Deng of South Sudan characterized this attitude as, "Let's just take that [success in Liberia] and superimpose it." It doesn't work like that. That's a problem."[10] Likewise, most donors properly demand that efforts be made to measure progress toward identified objectives. It is important to make project managers accountable. But sometimes

Effectiveness," Trade Union Development Network (November 2011), http://www.aideffectiveness.org/busanhlf4/images/stories/hlf4/TU_messages_to_Busan_EN.pdf; "The Tunis Consensus: Targeting Effective Development," African Development Bank, NEPAD Planning and Coordinating Agency, and African Union Commission (November 2010), http://www.afdb.org/fileadmin/uploads/afdb/Documents/Generic-Documents/Tunis_Consensus_3mars.pdf; "The Monrovia Roadmap on Peacebuilding and Statebuilding," International Dialogue on Peacebuilding and Statebuilding (July 2011), http://www.oecd.org/dataoecd/23/24/48345560.pdf.

8. Rubén Zamora, remarks at *Rethinking Civilian Stabilization and Reconstruction*, CSIS conference, July 16, 2013, Washington, D.C.

9. Husain Haqqani, remarks at *Rethinking Civilian Stabilization and Reconstruction*, CSIS conference, July 16, 2013, Washington, D.C.

10. William Deng Deng, remarks at *Rethinking Civilian Stabilization and Reconstruction*, CSIS conference, July 16, 2013, Washington, D.C.

they are not realistic about what "metrics" can do for them: measurable indicators are only proxies for real-world success. If donors forget that, Zamora pointed out, "You start to be a slave to the indicator, working for the indicator and not for the country."

Overcoming Operational Challenges in South Sudan

Places such as South Sudan are complex: a new country, recently broken off from its northern namesake, facing bilateral disputes with Sudan over oil and borders, transnational armed groups operating in its territory, ethnic tensions and violence, unstable neighbors, and humanitarian challenges, while struggling to demobilize former combatants, build government accountability and capacity, and more generally establish peace and stability. Into this complex environment steps the international community, which adds a large number of organizations, projects, procedures, and demands upon a small number of government ministers and civil society leaders. South Sudan's situation is the kind for which donor commitments to coordination and harmonization with local conditions and priorities are intended.

The South Sudan response helps to illustrate the constraints and practices that make it difficult for donors to meet commitments and overcome the challenges inherent to complex situations. A fairly basic problem is one of disagreement: different actors on the donor and recipient sides simply do not agree with each other on development goals, time frames, politics, perspectives on the conflicts, and other issues. Aid agencies have budget constraints as well, not just in the amount of resources available, but in how those resources may be spent. Formal authorities and bureaucratic inefficiencies make it difficult for aid officials and implementers to coordinate effectively with local and international development partners and to have the flexibility to adapt programming to changing circumstances. Legal and ideological impediments limit engagement with certain religious and military groups, even those understood as being critical contributors to stability. Short in-country rotations make it difficult to form and maintain the personal relationships that are necessary for building trust between donor and recipient personnel.

These issues are not specific to South Sudan. Certainly, the international community's support has made South Sudan's transition significantly more effective than it otherwise would have been, a point made clear repeatedly during the panel. As these and other panelists throughout the day argued, there has been real progress in the way some donor organizations operate more generally. But the shortcomings that remain are telling. A decade after the first high-level forum for aid effectiveness, so many commitments and declarations have been made—and so many lessons collected—without being institutionalized that an increasing number of donor and recipient professionals are questioning whether the focus on aid effectiveness should shift more firmly toward studies of the institutions, procedures, authorities, cultures, practices, and, most broadly, political economy of donor organizations.

Reflections on the State of the Field and the Future of Stabilization

The final speakers—Rob Jenkins, USAID's acting deputy assistant administrator of the Bureau for Democracy, Conflict, and Humanitarian Affairs and formerly the longstanding director of the Office of Transition Initiatives (OTI), and Rick Barton, assistant secretary of state for the Bureau of Conflict and Stabilization Operations—offered views about the field that were generally consistent with the main themes that had arisen throughout the day. Among those themes were the importance of respecting local communities and institutions and their priorities, remaining flexible and willing to take risks in implementation, balancing short-term demands with long-term objectives, customizing interventions to local conditions, and collecting and sharing data about the effectiveness of different projects and approaches. Both speakers addressed the question of why donor organizations have had difficulty institutionalizing lessons. In addition to not being given the resources needed to make the changes demanded, many donor organizations are too risk-averse to try anything that would set a precedent. Still, U.S. agencies involved in this field should get some credit for the improvements they have made over the past decade, as discussed in earlier panels, including improvements in conflict prevention.

Rob Jenkins observed that "the field" itself is rather ill-defined: it has no name and so sometimes is referred to by one of its many subdisciplines, including stabilization, reconstruction, peace building, transition, consolidation, and nation building, among others. In general, all of these subdisciplines seek to reduce violence, manage or mitigate conflicts, and build stable institutions to encourage human well being and peace—much more, in other words, than mere stability. But within and across these subdisciplines there are many different visions for how to accomplish these things and different understandings of how long it takes to accomplish them.

In his closing keynote address, Rick Barton offered a series of "provocations," or suggestions, for how the individuals and organizations involved in this field can make their work more effective:

- The donor community needs to adapt to the changing nature of conflict and public attitudes about intervention. Conflicts today are much more like popular revolts than organized wars. Elites have more difficulty directing movements and dictating tactics than they once did, so changes happen more quickly and violence can spiral out of the control of the elites who started it. At least in the near term, conflict and post-conflict work will probably not take place in the context of large-scale military interventions such as those in Afghanistan and Iraq, which suggests that the field might be entering a "golden moment for civilians"—if the needed civilian capacities can be developed.
- To build capacities, policy and implementation need to work much more hand-in-hand than they do today, whereby the State Department sets policies that other

agencies and contractors are expected to implement. Many implementers know that the changes policymakers often want to achieve can take a generation or more and that there is an immediate need for signs of progress. Both policymakers and implementers need to demand—and accept—incremental progress both early on and throughout the entire period of the intervention. As Barton observed about the relationship between the "grass roots" of the field and policymakers: "Grass doesn't grow without sun and rain, or it turns to hay. But sun and rain without grass is just mud."

- The system as it stands now is not well suited to uniting policy and implementation. Special envoys and offices in charge of coordinating and convening do not have the decisive authority that is required to move all the disparate parts of policy and implementation toward the same direction. The National Security Staff is too small and overstretched to focus the attention that is required. Barton does not think a new organization is needed, only that whatever agency is best suited to the nature of a particular contingency should be designated the lead agency and given decisive authority over other offices.

- Individual crises should be analyzed based primarily on the issues and themes in play, not on the region they are in, as is usually the case today. For example, Angola's civil war had more lessons that were relevant to the conflict in Serbia than it did for the conflicts in the Democratic Republic of Congo (DRC), even though DRC and Angola are in the same region; Haiti had more to teach about the DRC than Angola, even though they are on different hemispheres. Regional bureaus and experts tend to have more influence than functional offices and thematic experts. Deep regional knowledge is clearly important, but if that is the primary "analytic lens" though which policy is made, opportunities for progress will be missed.

Finally, Barton and Jenkins both emphasized the need for donors to definitively change their views on local ownership, which is recognized far more in writing than in practice. Country ministries and local communities are usually willing and capable of identifying what is most needed and what is most important, while donors tend to offer what is most familiar or most available. Marginalized groups and "silent majorities" also need to be consulted more. In many armed conflicts, most people do not support any of the warring factions, but their voices are drowned out by much better organized government and opposition figures. Without consulting locals to identify their most important problems and then committing to helping solve them, donors are not likely to succeed. The enormity and complexity of stabilization and reconstruction tasks should be approached with humility.

Themes and Recommendations

Many of the themes that emerged over the course of the day's conference should be familiar to anyone who has been in the stabilization and reconstruction field for more than a few years. Nonetheless, several of the more prominent themes are worth highlighting because they suggest some new directions the field is starting to take.

- *Unit of analysis.* The stabilization and reconstruction field is still sometimes referred to as nation building or state building. It is increasingly recognized, however, that national-level factors are not always the most relevant to ending conflict or building peace. Local actors and conditions are critically important (and differ from place to place in the same country) and foreign powers sometimes have more influence on the course, length, or severity of the conflict than national political leaders. The unit of analysis in research and policymaking is shifting to capture more subnational and transnational—and at times great power—dynamics.

- *Data.* It follows from the previous point that more data are needed at the local and regional levels. As more data are geocoded—tagged with information about location—studies of peace and conflict will become more precise, which will help policymakers target interventions more intelligently. But that will happen only if organizations geocode any data they collect and share it more openly. A number of speakers at the conference pointed out that good data, good indicators, and evidence from the field are vital for effective action.

- *Indicators.* As important as good data is, it cannot lead to good policy unless it represents something meaningful. Relevant indicators for progress and success are difficult to devise and collect, although progress is being made toward recognizing that "input" and "output" indicators cannot be proxies for desired outcomes. Good indicators are needed, but care must be taken that projects do not become beholden to them: an indicator is only a proxy for a real-world outcome. Those who monitor and evaluate projects therefore should be aware that a project can meet an indicator without having achieved success.

- *Planning.* Because situations in contingency environments can change so quickly, flexibility and improvisation are extremely important features of implementation, but they should not overshadow the continued importance of good planning. Plans should not be immovable objects once developed. Instead, a robust planning process is needed so that a broad range of considerations and potential complications can at least be accounted for. Some donor organizations are finding ways to make room for riskier projects. A portfolio of projects, for example, can include a mix of tried-and-true approaches (hopefully not mere blueprints) and field experiments to test innovative ideas and project designs on the ground. Some projects should start small and grow as they succeed; those that need to be launched at a larger scale should be very clear about how all the elements fit together. In all cases, there should be a clear understanding of what a project is designed to accomplish—and what makes the planners believe it can work.

- *Stability versus change.* Stability can bring peace in the short term, but change is needed to maintain peace in the long run. Short-term stability is needed before changes can be made for long-term peace, but the actions and effects of stabilization are not always compatible with the ability to make the changes needed to build peace. Donors are beginning to recognize that these tensions, while constant, can only be addressed if those carrying out short-term efforts are in constant contact with those carrying out longer-term efforts, constantly monitoring conditions and needs as they change.

- *Disruption.* Ultimately, foreign assistance is designed to be disruptive: the intention is to disrupt broken systems and improve their functioning. But it does not always improve things: sometimes aid is absorbed without effect and sometimes it harms the functioning of the system it was intended to help. To militate against counterproductive disruptions, humility and respect for local concerns and priorities are required, as are adaptability, flexibility, and skepticism. Local voices are important even though they may be biased. Key relationships need to be fostered, not just with national and local elites, but with others whose voices are not usually heard, whether they be oppressed minorities or silent majorities.

- *Gender.* Implementing partners of both the donor and recipient country tend to be male-dominated, although young professionals in this field are increasingly female. Systematic research and anecdotal evidence have suggested recently that many development projects are more effective when led by women in the communities that are the intended beneficiaries. Research on the role of gender in conflict, by contrast, has generally focused on women as victims. But there are growing bodies of research on women as perpetrators of violence and, importantly, women as peacemakers.

- *The private sector.* An increased focus on job creation and private-sector participation in international development has naturally led to a growing interest in how the private sector copes with violence and what role it can place in mediating or moderating conflict.

- *Urban violence.* Urbanization is an inexorable trend worldwide and urban violence a growing area of concern for policymakers and topic for researchers.

Amid discussions of these themes and other topics, the key questions posed at the beginning of this report were addressed to varying degrees throughout the conference.

- *Can the United States prevent or end conflicts and protect its interests without using its military?* Even using its military, the United States has only a limited ability to influence the outcomes of complex crises. With aid and diplomacy, it cannot transform foreign societies or resolve their conflicts without the cooperation of influential local actors. Too many factors affect events in complex crises for any one actor to have decisive influence, and the United States is almost always constrained by logistical and political demands, including competing foreign policy priorities. But there are times when a smart mix of all tools at its disposal—with or without the threat of force—can be influential, if rarely decisive.

- *Do U.S. civilian institutions have the right mix of support, funding, and capabilities to respond to major crises and political transitions?* In a word, no—not at the same time, at least. Authorities regulating civilian efforts in relatively safe environments are not always well suited to complex contingency environments, when speed and flexibility are far more important for success; yet many of the same authorities regulate civilian work in both types of environment. Training, family support, and personnel rules often provide disincentives to doing work in this field—either at all or, in some cases, for the lengths of time needed to build the expertise and relationships required to be effective. Funding is usually inadequate relative to the demands being made—but at times can be excessive relative to what can reasonably be absorbed. And too often the greatest amount of money is budgeted (and required to be spent) early on, when public interest in the crisis is high but the capacity to spend it responsibly does not yet exist. Budgets then decline over time as the capacity grows but public interest wanes. The need to use contractors adds a layer of complexity as well. Contracting officers are not always educated or sympathetic about the demands of contingency environments. Contractors often work with vague guidance, and oversight is sometimes too loose to hold them accountable and sometimes so stringent it encourages risk aversion. Moreover, effectiveness and accountability are at risk when work needs to be done in places that are too dangerous for outsiders to implement or monitor. Finally, the public, political leaders, and sometimes practitioners themselves often have unrealistically high expectations for what can be accomplished with the resources, support, and capabilities available.

- *What do civilian institutions do well? What needs improvement? Where is more support for civilian capabilities needed?* This report has touched on many of the answers to these questions, and the previous paragraph identifies some of the areas where more support is needed. Assessments have improved significantly over the past decade, accounting for more local dynamics, nonstate actors, political economy, and root causes. But how to incorporate all of that information into plans and (especially when improvisation is needed) into practice remains a challenge. Lessons from project evaluations and outside research are abundant, and more geocoded data are being collected in ways that make more sophisticated analysis possible. But evaluations and data are not always shared. If information were more open, significantly more and better research could be done to understand the subtle differences that influence effectiveness in different contexts. There is a growing recognition that ending and recovering from conflict need to be processes that are led by locals—but this too often continues to be recognized in word more than deed. Probably the most important way the civilian stabilization and reconstruction field could be better supported is with a set of authorities and institutions designed specifically for the demands faced in places affected by conflict, violence, and fragility, where normal processes and practices in development have proven ineffective.

- *What should practitioners and researchers do to help the United States institutionalize the right lessons from history and on-the-ground experience?* First is education. It turns out that the lessons and effective practices familiar to many practitioners and researchers are not at all familiar to most legislators, elected officials, political appointees, the public, and even a significant population of the donor organizations themselves, including contracting officers, human resources staff, personnel security chiefs, budget analysts, and others who have significant influence over what can be done on the ground. Second is patience. A lot of different offices and organizations have a stake in what gets done on the ground, and it takes a lot of work to coordinate, build consensus (or at least agreement), and convince risk-averse bureaucracies to take a chance on an approach that is not the boilerplate they are used to. Things take longer than they should, and that probably will not change anytime soon. Third is research. Evaluations and case studies often find that a project failure can be attributed to some factor that had not been accounted for or some action that had not been taken by the donor or implementing partner. The policy recommendation that naturally follows is to account for that factor or take that action in the future: better donor coordination, more country ownership, more due diligence, and so on. It would be more useful, however, if researchers would take an extra step and determine why that recommended factor or action had not been included in the project under study in the first place. Ownership, coordination, and so on are not new concepts, so why do donors so often overlook them? What is needed is more research on the political economy and bureaucratic cultures and processes of donor organizations to identify internal obstacles to effective aid practices and the institutionalization of lessons.

During his closing keynote, Rick Barton said that over the previous weeks he had taken to asking staff of different U.S. government agencies a simple question: "If you had a spectrum, and on one end of the spectrum is *native caution* and on the other end of the spectrum is *American ingenuity,* how many people here in this room . . . feel that they spend most of their time on the 'American ingenuity' side of the spectrum?" In all of the meetings where he asked this question, he said, "I have yet to have anybody raise their hand."[11]

At the lunchtime panel, William Deng introduced a different spectrum. Donors, "and especially the United States," he said, "have two P's on the extremes. One P is *passive*. . . . You give money to one country [then] remain passive, saying, . . . 'Don't worry.'" In his experience, donors do not focus enough on preventing conflict during periods when potentially destabilizing dynamics can still be managed. "And the other P is *panic!* 'My god, things are messed up!'" he said, suggesting that donors tend to take preconflict dynamics seriously a little too late, after the opportunity to take simple (and inexpensive) preventive action has passed, and then they have to expand intervention significantly or withdraw entirely. "But I think there is another P in between: *pragmatic*. That would make the third P, [and it] is not existent in your languages. You've got to be pragmatic. [When] you come to a country, you've got to realize they have their own political understanding."[12] Insiders, in

11. Frederick Barton, remarks at *Rethinking Civilian Stabilization and Reconstruction*, CSIS conference, July 16, 2013, Washington, D.C.

12. William Deng Deng, remarks at *Rethinking Civilian Stabilization and Reconstruction*, CSIS conference, July 16, 2013, Washington, D.C.

other words, have a far more realistic understanding of what can be achieved than outsiders, who too often arrive with grandiose ideas about transforming ministries, conflicts, political systems, or societies.

American ingenuity and American pragmatism: two of the most important defining characteristics of the United States since its independence from Great Britain. They are what helped build the American economy into the global powerhouse it is today, and what enabled the United States to enter the world stage and become a political superpower.

But they are not the defining characteristics of the stabilization and reconstruction field today.

Certainly there are pockets of brilliance, savvy individuals who know how to navigate complex contingency environments as well as they know how to navigate their own bureaucracies, and innovative projects that demonstrate what can be accomplished with the right combination of partnership, prioritization, creativity, resources, and accountability.

But ingenious and pragmatic professionals do not enter this field—and smart policymakers do not deploy them—to mainly apply familiar solutions to difficult problems while having only the occasional opportunity to innovate. There needs to be a policy and institutional environment in which innovation, experimentation, and flexibility—along with accountability—are the rules and not the exceptions. There is a reason complex crises and armed conflicts are sometimes called "contingencies": uncertainties, accidents, and luck define these situations, and they cannot be fully planned for in advance. Responding to them requires some planning but they also require a good dose of improvisation and a pragmatic understanding of institutional, financial, social, political, and cultural constraints of the communities into which donors intervene. For that to happen, important aspects of the stabilization and reconstruction field need to be rethought and perhaps approached with a bit more pragmatism and ingenuity.

Appendix A. Conference Agenda

CSIS, Tuesday, July 16, 2013

8:00–8:20 A.M. WELCOME AND OPENING REMARKS

- **John Hamre**, President and CEO, Center for Strategic and International Studies
- **Arthur Keys**, President and CEO, International Relief and Development
- **David M. Wall**, Senior Vice President, AECOM

8:20–8:40 A.M. IS AMERICA LOSING FAITH IN CIVILIAN POWER?

- **Robert D. Lamb**, Director, CSIS Program on Crisis, Conflict, and Cooperation

8:40–9:30 A.M. STABILIZATION AND RECONSTRUCTION BEYOND AFGHANISTAN

- **David Ignatius**, Associate Editor, *Washington Post*
- **James Dobbins**, U.S. Special Representative for Afghanistan and Pakistan

BREAK

9:45–11:45 A.M. U.S. SUPPORT TO TRANSITIONS

Moderator:

- **Johanna Mendelson Forman**, Senior Associate, CSIS Americas Program

Panel I: Colombia

- **Liliana Ayalde,** Deputy Assistant Secretary for Western Hemisphere Affairs, U.S. Department of State
- **Juan Pablo Franco Jiménez**, Director of Programs, IRD Colombia

Panel II: Liberia

- **John Blaney**, Senior Adviser, Deloitte Consulting
- **Sean McFate**, Vice President, TD International
- **Franklin Moore**, Senior Deputy Assistant Administrator for Africa, USAID

BREAK

12:15–1:30 P.M. WORKING WITH DONORS: A CONVERSATION WITH RECIPIENT-COUNTRY OFFICIALS

Moderator:

- **James Kunder,** Senior Resident Fellow, German Marshall Fund of the United States

Panelists:

- **William Deng Deng**, Chair, South Sudan National DDR Commission
- **Rubén Zamora**, Ambassador of El Salvador to the United States
- **Husain Haqqani**, Ambassador of Pakistan to the United States (2008–2011)

BREAK

1:45–2:45 P.M. OVERCOMING THE OPERATIONAL CHALLENGES TO DONOR COORDINATION

Moderator:

- **Andrew Natsios**, Executive Professor, Bush School of Government and Public Service

Panelists:

- **François Grignon**, Team Leader, Sudan/South Sudan, United Nations Department of Peacekeeping Operations (UN DPKO)
- **Jason Matus**, Senior Sudan Coordinator, AECOM
- **Jonathan Temin**, Director, Horn of Africa Program, Centers of Innovation, U.S. Institute of Peace (USIP)

2:45–3:15 P.M. OBSERVATIONS ABOUT THE STATE OF THE FIELD

- **Robert Jenkins**, Acting Deputy Assistant Administrator, USAID Bureau for Democracy, Conflict, and Humanitarian Assistance (DCHA) and Executive Director of the Syria Task Force
- **Robert D. Lamb**, Director, CSIS Program on Crisis, Conflict, and Cooperation

3:15–4:00 P.M. KEYNOTE ADDRESS: THE FUTURE OF STABILIZATION

- **Frederick "Rick" Barton**, Assistant Secretary for Conflict and Stabilization Operations, U.S. Department of State

Appendix B. Speaker Biographies

John Hamre

Dr. Hamre was elected president and chief executive officer (CEO) of CSIS in January 2000 and named Pritzker Chair in December 2012. Before joining CSIS, he served as the 26th U.S. deputy secretary of defense. Prior to holding that post, he was the under secretary of defense (comptroller) from 1993 to 1997. As comptroller, Dr. Hamre was the principal assistant to the secretary of defense for the preparation, presentation, and execution of the defense budget and management improvement programs. In 2007 Secretary of Defense Robert Gates appointed Dr. Hamre to serve as chairman of the Defense Policy Board. Before serving in the Department of Defense, Dr. Hamre worked for 10 years as a professional staff member of the Senate Armed Services Committee. During that time, he was primarily responsible for the oversight and evaluation of procurement, research, and development programs, defense budget issues, and relations with the Senate Appropriations Committee. From 1978 to 1984, Dr. Hamre served in the Congressional Budget Office, where he became its deputy assistant director for national security and international affairs. In that position, he oversaw analysis and other support for committees in both the House of Representatives and the Senate. Dr. Hamre received his Ph.D., with distinction, in 1978 from the School of Advanced International Studies at Johns Hopkins University in Washington, D.C., where his studies focused on international politics and economics and U.S. foreign policy. In 1972, he received his B.A., with high distinction, from Augustana College in Sioux Falls, South Dakota, emphasizing political science and economics. The following year he studied as a Rockefeller fellow at the Harvard Divinity School in Cambridge, Massachusetts.

Arthur Keys

Dr. Keys is the president and CEO of IRD. He has over 30 years of experience with domestic and international humanitarian assistance, economic development, and food/agriculture programs. His expertise spans a number of nongovernmental organizations as well as private consultancy. Dr. Keys has extensive experience partnering with major U.S. and international development agencies to provide humanitarian relief and assistance to the neediest parts of the world. Since founding IRD in 1998, Dr. Keys has overseen the distribution of more than $1.75 billion in humanitarian assistance to Asia, Africa, Latin America, Eastern Europe, the Middle East, and the United States Gulf Coast. Dr. Keys was previously the executive director of Interfaith Impact for Justice and Peace, the secretary for public ministries of the United Church Board for Homeland Ministries, and the president of the consulting firm Keys and Associates. Dr. Keys is a native of Washington, Pennsylvania. He has a doctorate from Emory University and a master of divinity from Yale University. He received his bachelor's degree from Bethany College. He is currently a member of the Board of Trustees at Bethany. He was awarded an honorary doctorate in humane letters from Bethany. He is also the recipient of the William Sloane Coffin '56 Award for Justice and Peace given annually by Yale Divinity School and was honored in Atlanta by the Emory University Alumni Board with the 2009 Emory Medal for his many years of humanitarian service. Dr. Keys is fluent in Serbo-Croatian. He is married and has three children.

David M. Wall

Mr. Wall, senior vice president of AECOM International Development, has more than 20 years of experience providing senior level management and technical direction, in the planning, monitoring, coordination, and reporting of reconstruction and rehabilitation activities as part of international development programs. Specializing in economic reform, he has served as a technical adviser on several missions for the World Bank, Asian Development Bank, and USAID, developing economic restructuring programs. Mr. Wall has worked extensively in the Middle East, including his work as the technical director at the USAID Office of Iraq Affairs, where he provided strategic leadership and guidance for mission critical projects in support of U.S. efforts focused on Iraq reconstruction, democratization, and stability. Currently, as the senior vice president for programs at AECOM International Development, Mr. Wall oversees all of AECOM's international development programs spanning economic growth, governance, crisis stabilization, global climate change, water, energy, and infrastructure. Furthermore, he has hands-on experience presenting and meeting with key USG decisionmakers including acting as USAID/Iraq representative during the 2008 CENTCOM assessment as well as joint campaign plan reviews for Iraq in 2007–2008. He has a proven record in senior line management and boardroom strategic consulting, combined with a global background in financial services industry throughout the Middle East, the Americas, Europe, and the Pacific Rim.

Robert D. Lamb

Dr. Lamb is a senior fellow and director of the Program on Crisis, Conflict, and Cooperation at CSIS and a research scholar at the Center for International and Security Studies at the University of Maryland. Dr. Lamb studies governance and development amid conflict, with an emphasis on hybrid political systems and complex crises. He has presented his work to policymakers and experts throughout the United States and in Afghanistan, Colombia, France, Germany, Greece, India, Korea, Pakistan, Romania, Russia, Sweden, and the United Kingdom. A former Defense Department strategist, he has developed tools to help policymakers pay more attention to local governance and informal systems in places that terrorist, criminal, and insurgent networks use as safe havens. As a doctoral candidate, he spent a year in Colombia developing new methods for studying gang governance, violence, and legitimacy in the stateless slums of Medellín. He earned a Ph.D. in policy studies from the University of Maryland School of Public Policy in a program combining security, economics, and ethics. He received a B.A. in interdisciplinary studies from Gettysburg College, spent half a year in Nicaragua with a microdevelopment project, then worked for nine years as an editor and journalist, winning a National Press Club award in 2001, before changing careers after 9/11.

David Ignatius

Mr. Ignatius writes a twice-a-week foreign affairs column in the *Washington Post* and contributes to the PostPartisan blog. Ignatius has also written eight spy novels: *Bloodmoney* (2011), *The Increment* (2009), *Body of Lies* (2007), *The Sun King* (1999), *A Firing Offense* (1997), *The Bank of Fear* (1994), *SIRO* (1991), and *Agents of Innocence* (1987). *Body of Lies* was made into a 2008 film starring Leonardo DiCaprio and Russell Crowe. Ignatius joined the *Post* in 1986 as editor of its Sunday Outlook section. In 1990 he became foreign editor and in 1993 assistant managing editor for business news. He began writing his column in 1998 and continued even during a three-year stint as executive editor of the *International Herald Tribune* in Paris. Earlier in his career, Ignatius was a reporter for the *Wall Street Journal*, covering at various times the steel industry, the Justice Department, the CIA, the Senate, the Middle East, and the State Department. Ignatius grew up in Washington, D.C., and studied political theory at Harvard College and economics at Kings College, Cambridge. He currently lives in Washington, D.C., with his wife and three daughters.

James Dobbins

Ambassador Dobbins was appointed by Secretary of State John Kerry as the special representative for Afghanistan and Pakistan on May 10, 2013. Prior to this appointment, Ambassador Dobbins served as director of the RAND International Security and Defense Policy Center. He has held State Department and White House posts, including assistant secretary of state for Europe, special assistant to the president, special adviser to the president and secretary of state for the Balkans, and ambassador to the European Community. Dobbins has had numerous crisis management and diplomatic troubleshooting assignments as the Bill Clinton and George W. Bush administrations' special envoy for Afghanistan, Kosovo, Bosnia, Haiti, and Somalia. His diplomatic assignments included the withdrawal of American forces from Somalia, the American-led multilateral intervention in Haiti, the stabilization and reconstruction of Bosnia, and the North Atlantic Treaty Organization (NATO) intervention in Kosovo. In the wake of September 11, 2001, he was named as the Bush administration's representative to the Afghan opposition with the task of putting together and installing a broadly based successor to the Taliban regime. He represented the United States at the Bonn Conference that established the new Afghan government, and on December 16, 2001, he raised the flag over the newly reopened U.S. embassy.

Johanna Mendelson Forman

Dr. Mendelson Forman is a senior associate with Americas Program at CSIS, where she works on renewable energy, the Americas, civil-military relations, and post-conflict reconstruction. A former codirector of the Post-Conflict Reconstruction Project, she has written extensively on security-sector reform in conflict states, economic development in postwar societies, the role of the United Nations in peace operations, and energy security. In 2003 she participated in a review of the post-conflict reconstruction effort of the Coalition Provisional Authority in Iraq as part of a CSIS team. Dr. Mendelson Forman also brings experience in the world of philanthropy, having served as the director of peace, security, and human rights at the UN Foundation. She has held senior positions in the U.S. government at the U.S. Agency for International Development, the Bureau for Humanitarian Response, and the Office of Transition Initiatives, as well as at the World Bank's Post Conflict Unit. She has been a senior fellow with the Association of the U.S. Army and a guest scholar at the U.S. Institute of Peace. Most recently, she served as an adviser to the UN Mission in Haiti. She holds adjunct faculty appointments at American University and Georgetown University. Dr. Mendelson Forman is a member of the Council on Foreign Relations and serves on the advisory boards of Women in International Security and the Latin American Security Network (known by its Spanish acronym, RESDAL). She holds a J.D. from Washington College of Law at American University, a Ph.D. in Latin American history from Washington University, St. Louis, and a master's of international affairs, with a certificate of Latin America studies, from Columbia University in New York. She is fluent in Spanish and Portuguese.

Liliana Ayalde

Ambassador Ayalde is a career minister serving as the deputy assistant secretary of state for Western Hemisphere affairs, covering Cuba, Central America, and the Caribbean. She previously served as the USAID senior deputy assistant administrator in the Bureau for Latin America and the Caribbean. She served as U.S. ambassador to Paraguay from 2008 to 2011. Ambassador Ayalde started her foreign service career in 1982 in Bangladesh and has accumulated more than 28 years of experience in diplomacy and development, most of this in the Western Hemisphere. Ambassador Ayalde has served in Guatemala and Nicaragua overseeing growing development assistance programs. In 1993 she was named deputy director for the Office of Central American Affairs in USAID's Latin America and Caribbean Bureau, becoming director in 1995 during the peace process in Central America. She returned to Nicaragua as deputy director for USAID and in 1997 was assigned as mission director for USAID/Bolivia. Between 2005 and 2008, she served as mission director for USAID/Colombia, during which time she had responsibility for the development assistance portfolio under Plan Colombia. Ambassador Ayalde holds a bachelor of arts degree from American University in international studies and a master's degree in international public health from Tulane University. She is fluent in Spanish and Portuguese and has a working knowledge of French.

Juan Pablo Franco Jiménez

Mr. Jiménez is the operations director of International Relief and Development (IRD) in Colombia, working in areas where armed conflict is still intense, to support the government in providing assistance to victims of forced displacement. Before IRD, he worked for seven years in the Colombian government, first as part of an interagency team set up to coordinate more than 10 ministries and agencies for the delivery of public services and goods in territories recovered by the army and police. He later came back to government as the director of victim assistance and reparation in charge of nationwide operations to register victims, deliver humanitarian assistance, coordinate access to other services, return displaced families to safe areas, and implement massive administrative reparation programs for more than four million victims of armed conflict. He was also a permanent delegate of the high presidential adviser for social action and international cooperation in the National Reparation and Reconciliation Commission and participated in the drafting and approval of the new Victims Law in 2011. He is an industrial engineer and political scientist, specialist in government and public policy, and holds a master's in public affairs from Science Po Paris.

John Blaney

Ambassador Blaney currently works for Deloitte Consulting, having just concluded his elected term as cochair of Deloitte's Luminary Advisory Board. As U.S. ambassador to Liberia (2002–2005), Ambassador Blaney ended Liberia's 14-year civil war on the battlefield, and was a key architect of Liberia's postwar stabilization program, including regime transition to the election of 2005. For those successes he received the President's Distinguished Honor Award, the Secretary of State's Distinguished Honor Award, and the Order of Redemption. Prior to that Ambassador Blaney had many assignments as a senior member of the U.S. Foreign Service, notably as the State Department's country director for Southern Africa, U.S. deputy representative to the Economic and Social Council (ECOSOC) of the United Nations, minister counselor in Moscow during the disintegration period of the Soviet Union, and earlier, as principal author and a negotiator of the first nuclear arms control agreement with the Union of Soviet Socialist Republics (USSR), the U.S.-USSR Nuclear Risk Reduction Centers Agreement. He also worked on both Strategic Arms Reduction Talks (START) and Intermediate Nuclear Forces (INF) talks, and was charge d'affaires in South Africa. Ambassador Blaney is an economist as well and worked earlier in his career at the U.S. Treasury Department and more recently on Wall Street as a political and economic adviser. A former U.S. Army officer and teacher at West Point, his degrees are from Syracuse and Georgetown universities.

Sean McFate

Dr. McFate is vice president of TD International, which he joined in 2012. He brings over 20 years of public, private, and nonprofit sector experience. Previously he was an assistant professor at the National Defense University at Fort McNair, where he taught grand strategy to senior military and civilian leaders from around the world. He was also a Bernard L. Schwartz Fellow at the New America Foundation and a director at the Bipartisan Policy Center, both think tanks in Washington, D.C. Before working in academia and policy, Dr. McFate worked in the private sector. He was a program manager for DynCorp International, a New York Stock Exchange–listed company that provides technical services for the U.S. government. There he designed and managed unique programs in Africa, such as building Liberia's army "from the ground up" after its 14-year civil war. He was also an associate at Booz Allen Hamilton and a business adviser at BearingPoint, now part of Deloitte Consulting. Prior to working in the private sector, he served as a U.S. Army officer and paratrooper in the 82nd Airborne Division. After the military, he advised Amnesty International on human rights and armed conflict. Dr. McFate has published articles in *Foreign Policy, African Affairs, Military Review, Royal United Services Institute Journal,* and *Review of African Political Economy.* He has authored six book chapters in edited volumes on foreign affairs, special reports for the U.S. Institute of Peace and the Stanley Foundation, and was a contributor to *The Encyclopedia of Intelligence and Counterintelligence* and *War Crimes and Trials: A Historical Encyclopedia.* He served on the editorial board of *Millennium: Journal of International Studies* (Sage Publications). Dr. McFate is an adjunct social scientist at the RAND Corporation, and an adjunct professor at the National Defense University. Dr. McFate holds double B.A.s from Brown University, an M.P.P. from Harvard University's Kennedy School of Government, and a Ph.D. in international relations from the London School of Economics.

Franklin Moore

A career member of the Senior Executive Service, Mr. Moore is the deputy assistant administrator of the U.S. Agency for International Development's Bureau for Africa, which provided $6.4 billion in assistance to 49 African countries in 2011. Mr. Moore also served in this position from January 2008 to July 2010. Prior to this appointment, Mr. Moore served in Rome as USAID's senior development counselor and senior adviser to the U.S. ambassador to Rome-based UN organizations from July 2010 to December 2012. Mr. Moore was director of the Office of Environment and Science Policy within the agency's Bureau for Economic Growth, Agriculture and Trade from 2002 to 2008, and he served as the acting deputy assistant administrator and director for the agency's Global Center for the Environment. Prior to joining USAID in 1998, Mr. Moore held positions in the areas of agriculture, environment, and national resource management with the U.S. Environmental Protection Agency; with Africare in Zimbabwe; and with the Peace Corps and as a lecturer at Virginia State University and the University of Science and Technology in Kumasi, Ghana. Mr. Moore has a bachelor's degree in economics with a minor in art history from Yale University. He received a master's degree in agricultural economics, as well as a certificate in African studies from the University of Wisconsin–Madison, and he studied for a Ph.D. in development studies at the University of Wisconsin–Madison. Mr. Moore has lived and worked in both West and Southern Africa; he has worked in approximately 40 countries overseas.

James Kunder

Mr. Kunder is a senior resident fellow at the German Marshall Fund of the United States (GMF). He advises on international development issues including the modernization of foreign assistance and the nexus between security and development. Previously, Mr. Kunder served as acting deputy administrator of the U.S. Agency for International Development (USAID), the U.S. government organization responsible for administering the U.S. foreign assistance programs. He has extensive government and private-sector experience in international development. Beginning in July 2004 at USAID, he served as assistant administrator for Asia and the Near East. Previously, from July 2002 to July 2004, he was the deputy assistant administrator for Asia and the Near East, and from January to May 2002 he was director for relief and reconstruction in Afghanistan. From 1987 to 1991 Mr. Kunder was deputy assistant administrator for external affairs at USAID. He then served as director of the agency's Office of U.S. Foreign Disaster Assistance from 1991 to 1993. From 1993 to 1996 he was vice president for program development at Save the Children Federation, an international nongovernmental organization dedicated to improving the lives of children in the United States and around the world. Mr. Kunder has also served as a legislative director in the U.S. House of Representatives, senior transportation analyst for the Commonwealth of Pennsylvania, and deputy director for the National Republican Senatorial Committee. He was an infantry platoon commander in the U.S. Marine Corps from 1970 to 1973. He has authored numerous articles on international humanitarian issues, peacekeeping, and crisis management.

William Deng Deng

Mr. Deng Deng has been the chairperson of the National DDR Commission since 2009. After fleeing Sudan, he received refugee status in Canada. He holds bachelor's and master's degrees from York University. He has worked in numerous conflict areas over the years. Mr. Deng Deng worked with the United Nations in Rwanda to initiate environmental rehabilitation with returning refugees and worked to negotiate with and reintegrate rebel fighters into society.

Rubén Zamora

Ambassador Zamora, El Salvador's ambassador to the United States, is an experienced Salvadoran politician identified as a social democrat and remembered for being the first candidate to the presidency (1994) for a leftist coalition between the Farabundo Martí National Liberation Front (FMLN in Spanish) and Democratic Convergence (CD in Spanish) after the signing of the Peace Accords (1992). In 1999, he participated in the presidential elections as the United Democratic Center Party candidate, no longer in coalition with the FMLN Party. His career as a politician began in the 1970s when he was council member of the mayor's office in San Salvador, a post he held until 1972. In 1980 he was one of the founders of the Democratic Revolutionary Front Party, but during the civil war he was forced to leave the country. After his return to El Salvador in 1988, he helped to found the Democratic Convergence party, recognized as a leftist-center party that participated in the presidential elections in 1989 before the signing of the Peace Accords. He was a member of the Peace Commission (1991–1993) and the Legislative Assembly (1991–1994 and 1997–2000) and is currently a member of the Democratic Change Party. He was ambassador of El Salvador in India beginning in 2009 and in April 2013 was appointed ambassador to the United States. Ambassador Zamora graduated as an attorney at law at the University of El Salvador and later obtained a master's degree in political science at Essex University, England. He has been a guest professor at Stanford University and guest investigator at Notre Dame University and the Wilson Center. He has authored several books including *El Salvador: Wounds That Don't Heal: Postwar Political Parties* and *The Salvadoran Leftist Partisan: Between Entity and Power.*

Husain Haqqani

Ambassador Haqqani is a Pakistani scholar and public figure who most recently served as Pakistan's ambassador to the United States from 2008 to 2011. He is widely credited with managing a difficult partnership during a critical phase in the global war on terrorism. Haqqani started his public life as an Islamist student leader and has, over the years, emerged as a strong voice for democracy and civilian control of the military in Pakistan and an exponent of liberal values in the Muslim world. His distinguished career in government includes serving as an adviser to three Pakistani prime ministers, including Benazir Bhutto, who described him as a loyal friend in the last book she wrote before her assassination. He also served as Pakistan's ambassador to Sri Lanka in 1992–1993. Ambassador Haqqani is the author of the book *Pakistan between Mosque and Military* and hundreds of articles published in major international newspapers, magazines, and scholarly journals. He is currently senior fellow and director for South and Central Asia at the Hudson Institute. Haqqani also coedits the journal *Current Trends in Islamist Ideology* published by Hudson Institute's Center for Islam, Democracy and Future of the Muslim World. He is also director of the Center of International Relations and professor of the practice of international relations at Boston University.

Andrew Natsios

Mr. Natsios is an executive professor and Scowcroft Institute Fellow at the Bush School of Government and Public Service. Mr. Natsios was most recently a distinguished professor in the practice of diplomacy at Georgetown University and former administrator of the U.S. Agency for International Development (USAID). As USAID administrator from 2001 to 2006, Mr. Natsios managed reconstruction programs in Afghanistan, Iraq, and Sudan. He also served as U.S. special envoy to Sudan from 2006 to 2007. Now retired from the U.S. Army Reserve after 23 years, Mr. Natsios is a veteran of the Gulf War. From 1993 to 1998 he was vice president of World Vision USA, the largest faith-based nongovernmental organization in the world, with programs in 103 countries. Earlier in his career, Mr. Natsios served in the Massachusetts House of Representatives and as the chief financial and administrative officer of the Commonwealth of Massachusetts. He also served as CEO of Boston's Big Dig, the largest construction project in American history, after a cost overrun scandal. He is the author of three books: *U.S. Foreign Policy and the Four Horsemen of the Apocalypse* (1997); *The Great North Korean Famine* (2001); and *Sudan, South Sudan and Darfur: What Everyone Needs to Know* (2012).

François Grignon

Dr. Grignon is currently the team leader for Sudan/South Sudan in the UN Department of Peacekeeping Operations. He holds a Ph.D. in political science from the University Montesquieu Bordeaux IV and graduated from the Institut d'Etudes Politiques in Paris. Former researcher on East Africa and deputy director of the French Institute of Research in Africa (IFRA-Nairobi), Dr. Grignon led the Central Africa International Crisis Group (ICG) project between 2000 and 2004, specializing in the peace process in Burundi and the Democratic Republic of Congo, before joining the office of the Special Representative of the Secretary-General directing the UN Mission in Congo (MONUC), where he established and led the integrated risk analysis and political and security threats unit (Joint Mission Analysis Cell, JMAC). He then joined ICG to head the Africa Programme from 2007 to 2010.

Jason Matus

Mr. Matus has been the senior coordinator for the Sudan and South Sudan transition and conflict mitigation programs at AECOM since 2010. He has over 19 over years of experience in Sudan and South Sudan working on humanitarian, conflict mitigation, and peacebuilding programs with the United Nations; USAID; U.S. Special Envoy's Office; the European Commission; a donor working group on Abyei, Southern Kordofan, and Blue Nile; the World Bank; and various nongovernmental organizations. He has served as an adviser, coordinator, livelihood analyst, and project manager in support of peace initiatives related to the Comprehensive Peace Agreement and post-secession stabilization efforts within and between the two countries. For the last 13 years, Mr. Matus has focused primarily on the border areas between Sudan and South Sudan. Mr. Matus received his master of professional studies in international development from Cornell University.

Jonathan Temin

Mr. Temin is the director of the Horn of Africa Program at the U.S. Institute of Peace (USIP), which focuses on helping to end Sudan, South Sudan, and Somalia's multiple conflicts and to prevent new violence. Mr. Temin also follows developments elsewhere in sub-Saharan Africa. He travels to Sudan, South Sudan, and other countries in the region frequently to assess developments and meet with government officials, civil society leaders, and diplomats. Mr. Temin's commentary on African issues has been featured by, among other outlets, the BBC, Al Jazeera, *New York Times, Washington Post, Foreign Policy,* Voice of America, and National Public Radio. He has also testified before the U.S. Senate Committee on Foreign Relations on Sudan and South Sudan. Prior to joining USIP in January 2009, Mr. Temin spent five years with the nongovernmental organization CHF International designing development and peace-building programs throughout Africa and elsewhere. He has working experience in more than a dozen countries across Africa, Latin America, and Eastern Europe. Mr. Temin is the author of numerous articles focusing on Africa, conflict and governance which have appeared in, among other publications, *African Affairs, Review of African Political Economy, Journal of Peacebuilding and Development*, and the *Georgetown Journal of International Affairs*. He has also authored multiple reports for USIP. Mr. Temin holds a B.A. from Swarthmore College and an M.A. in international relations from the Johns Hopkins University School of Advanced International Studies. He is a former Fulbright Fellow in Ghana, where he worked with the Ghana Center for Democratic Development, monitoring media coverage of the 2000 elections.

Robert Jenkins

Mr. Jenkins is the director of USAID's Office of Transition Initiatives (OTI). Since April 2013 he has been the executive director of USAID's Syria Task Force and is also serving as acting deputy assistant administrator for USAID's Bureau for Democracy, Conflict, and Humanitarian Assistance. Prior to becoming director of OTI in October 2004, Mr. Jenkins served as OTI's operations coordinator and Iraq team leader. Mr. Jenkins joined OTI in March 1998 and has provided Washington-based support to OTI's programs in Iraq, Macedonia, Serbia and Montenegro, Kosovo, Sierra Leone, Liberia, and Nigeria. Prior to joining USAID, Mr. Jenkins designed and implemented emergency relief and recovery programs with World Vision International in southern Sudan and Sierra Leone. As a Thomas J. Watson Fellow he worked under Archbishop Desmond Tutu in Cape Town, South Africa, as a liaison between the Anglican Church's peace and justice office and township communities. His work included coordinating a network of political violence monitors and serving as an on-call independent observer, investigative monitor, and emergency crisis mediator. Mr. Jenkins holds a B.A in history and government from Bowdoin College.

Frederick "Rick" Barton

Ambassador Barton was sworn in as assistant secretary of state for conflict and stabilization operations and coordinator for reconstruction and stabilization on April 3, 2012. Ambassador Barton has worked to improve the U.S. and international response to conflict in more than 30 of the world's most unstable places. He led independent reviews of Iraq reconstruction; developed civilian strategies for Iraq, Sudan, and Sri Lanka; created new measurements of progress in Iraq and Afghanistan; and initiated path-breaking approaches to conflict reduction in Pakistan and Nigeria. He has served as codirector of the Post-Conflict Reconstruction Project at the Center for Strategic and International Studies (CSIS), deputy high commissioner of the UN Refugee Agency (UNHCR), and founding director of the U.S. Agency for International Development's Office of Transition Initiatives. Previously, Ambassador Barton served for nearly two years as the U.S. representative to the Economic and Social Council (ECOSOC) of the United Nations, working on development, peace building, climate change, and human rights. Ambassador Barton served on the CSIS Smart Power Commission, as an expert adviser to the Iraq Study Group, and as professor and lecturer at Princeton University's Woodrow Wilson School. He led conflict-related working groups at the U.S. Institute of Peace and for the Princeton Project on National Security. Ambassador Barton is a past chairperson of the Maine Democratic Party. He graduated from Harvard College in 1971 and earned his M.B.A. from Boston University in 1982. As the children of American diplomats, Ambassador Barton and his brothers lived in Argentina, Spain, the Dominican Republic, Bolivia, and Mexico. Married since 1975, Mr. Barton and his wife, Kit Lunney, have an adult daughter, Kacy, and live in Washington, D.C.

Appendix C. Summary of Proceedings

Summary Prepared by International Relief and Development (IRD)

Syria and Mali are not the first foreign conflicts the United States has tried to avoid intervening in militarily; nor will they be the last. Despite common beliefs, U.S. leaders rarely use military power to respond to foreign crises. When they do, it is only after exhausting civilian options. Do U.S. civilian institutions have the right mix of support, funding, and capabilities to respond to major crises and political transitions? Can the United States protect its interests and prevent conflicts without using its military? CSIS, IRD, and AECOM hosted a distinguished group of experts to take a deeper look at where the United States stands in its civilian capacity for reconstruction and stabilization.

Is America Losing Faith in Civilian Power?

- **Robert D. Lamb**, Director, CSIS Program on Crisis, Conflict, and Cooperation

This presentation highlighted a CSIS study showing that the United States has intervened in less than one-fifth of the world's 400 major protests, conflicts, and coups since 1989. When the United States does intervene, it uses civilian empowerment interventions, with military intervention as a last resort. The study also demonstrates that the demand for civilian-led response and civilian response tools often exceeds the supply, and civilian programs do not always benefit from the same levels of funding and support as their military counterparts for transition, stabilization, and reconstruction efforts. Development and stabilization activities do produce results, and those of us working in stabilization and reconstruction must be aware of lessons learned such as the following:

- We often do what we know rather than what is relevant; this does not usually work.
- Our perceptions of constraints may not necessarily be constraints in the local context.
- We must identify obstacles and reasons implementers are not applying lessons learned.
- The topic of "women as peacemakers" needs more attention.

- We must emphasize data collection and especially data sharing. Data collection should be gathered more efficiently, including global positioning system (GPS) tagging, and shared in a way that can be disaggregated.

Stabilization and Reconstruction beyond Afghanistan

- **David Ignatius**, Associate Editor, *Washington Post*
- **James Dobbins**, U.S. Special Representative for Afghanistan and Pakistan

This discussion reviewed the significant U.S. spending on stabilization and reconstruction and the achievements and shortcomings of the programs. Given that the model of sending large armies abroad to achieve stability has likely ended for the foreseeable future, the panelists raised the concern that USAID has become more of a contractor than an operator and questioned who among USAID, USIP, the Department of State, or other U.S. government entities are up to the task of prioritization and implementation of U.S. responses to fragility, conflict, and stabilization. Panelists also discussed the potential for rebranding USAID and increasing its funding to allow the agency to focus more on reconstruction and development.

The panel highlighted the importance of the transitions Afghanistan is facing, from externally funded to internally funded growth and from the Karzai government to another government. A peaceful transition is critical to the country's future. It is important to note that while the public here in the United States and in Europe judge elections in terms of process (i.e., were they "free and fair"?), Afghans are more concerned with the end results. Along that line, studies revealed that Afghans perceived the last elections to be fraudulent, but they were nevertheless happy with the results. The success of the next elections will depend on whether they produce a leader who can cross sectarian lines.

Afghanistan has been producing achievements. The country has seen a 15 percent increase in democratization indices, the highest in recent years among countries emerging from conflict. The government is delivering services, resulting in a doubled literacy rate and increased life expectancy. The government is also providing wireless and television access so people can participate in governance. Tax collection in Afghanistan is better than in Pakistan, and Afghanistan is more democratic than neighboring China, Tajikistan, and Uzbekistan, among others.

With regard to the fight against corruption, while identifying and criticizing corruption is necessary, it is also important to understand its causes. Institutions in Afghanistan are still less than 10 years old and do not inspire the same loyalty U.S. institutions do; rather, loyalties remain with family, neighbors, and tribes. To combat corruption, the U.S. partnership with Afghanistan should continue to focus on building competent, well-functioning institutions. Afghanistan demonstrates the lesson that a focus on eliminating networks like al Qaeda and the Taliban rather than bringing them into the discussions does not work. The United States will need to find ways to help fill the power gap as it withdraws in 2014. Civilian organizations and the military need to work together in support of stabilization; neither will be able to do the task on its own.

The panel presented the findings of a recent analysis of 20 countries emerging from conflict with U.S. and other international assistance over the past 10 years. Data were collected from Freedom House, World Bank, International Monetary Fund (IMF), and other publicly available sources. Of the 20 countries, 16 were "peaceful," meaning that the analysis showed positive trends in most indicators, including a faster economic growth rate than other countries. Afghanistan improved the fastest, in the top five in its level of economic growth, democratic governance, and health indicators. Successful stabilization depends on successful geopolitics and uniting the interests of competing patronage networks, as well as the consent of the host country when foreign troops come in, even if that consent follows a coerced agreement. The size of a country and the resources and incentives of the international community are also factors.

It was suggested that the stabilization efforts of the U.S. government might be made more effective by consolidating all civilian reconstruction programming as well as development projects being carried out across the government within one agency, along the lines of a "U.S. Agency for Reconstruction and Development," which would still be subordinate to the State Department because of the importance of geopolitics to stabilizing conflict zones.

According to many indicators, the world has become more peaceful and less threatened by catastrophic violence in modern years. For example, the number of people killed in wars, the number of refugees, and the number of violent conflicts are all down. The reductions may be slowing, however, which could indicate that the world may be emerging from this period of relative peace.

U.S. Support to Transitions in Colombia and Liberia

- **Liliana Ayalde,** Deputy Assistant Secretary for Western Hemisphere Affairs, U.S. Department of State
- **John Blaney**, Senior Adviser, Deloitte Consulting
- **Juan Pablo Franco Jiménez**, Director of Programs, IRD Colombia
- **Sean McFate**, Vice President, TD International
- **Franklin Moore**, Senior Deputy Assistant Administrator for Africa, USAID
- Moderator: **Johanna Mendelson Forman**, Senior Associate, CSIS Americas Program

Colombia and Liberia are examples of countries that have successfully emerged from conflict and represent the "end stage" of transition and stabilization efforts. The panel noted that there is no single recipe for a country to emerge from conflict but offered some lessons learned from Colombia and Liberia that may be generalizable. In the transition from stabilization to reconstruction and development, there is no definitive point where one ends and the other begins, and activities should occur simultaneously. What led to the war needs to be identified to find a pathway to stability: the war did not create the destabilization, the issues leading to the war did. Also, a return to what existed before the war is not sufficient. A longer-term vision is needed to create something better than what existed at the point of destabilization. Strategic wins are essential for creating legitimacy of a government and a semblance of return to normalcy, for example, getting streetlights turned back on.

We must also be realistic about progress indicators. For example, the continuing issue of internally displace persons (IDP) in Liberia may not indicate regression, as IDPs are migrating to cities at the same rate as the rest of the population. In Colombia, freedom to travel is a success indicator, as this freedom is based on indicators such as reduced levels of kidnappings. Another indicator is the number of mayors present in the municipalities they serve (at one time, more than 200 mayors did not live or work in their municipalities; today, most are in their communities). In addition, Colombia is "exporting" security: Colombian police are now training police forces in countries such as Mexico and Japan, and the police department has an international arm. Other Central American countries request Colombian training. However, Colombia is still in an ongoing, serious peace process. The Revolutionary Armed Forces of Colombia (FARC) still thrives in rural areas, police are still being killed in urban areas, and large numbers of displaced families are still arriving in urban areas.

COLOMBIA LESSONS LEARNED

The panel presented 10 lessons learned from a successful program in Colombia's Macarena region (a cocaine-rich area that was once dominated by the FARC):

1. A minimal level of security is required. Development does not bring security, and it is difficult to implement development without the support of security.

2. Host-country ownership and political will are prerequisites.

3. U.S. government assistance is a catalyst, but not the replacement, for the state. Geographic or technical areas should be identified where we can be the catalyst. In Macarena, at first the program provided 85 percent direct implementation, but the government came to the forefront and now implements the larger part of the programming.

4. A light footprint is better. Programs should brand the local government's success, with U.S. and implementer branding remaining in the background. This ensures citizens gain confidence in state institutions, which is essential to producing stabilization.

5. Act in the short term with a vision for transitioning to the long term. Immediate results are important for signaling change, but there needs to be a plan for how activities will progress to longer-term development.

6. Integration and sequencing of activities require intensive coordination and collaboration with the host-country government at national, regional, and local levels.

7. Take risks. For example, enter insecure areas, and when in those areas, be very hands-on at first.

8. Take an evidence-based approach with a robust monitoring and evaluation (M&E) system.

9. Undertake action research and redirect resources as needed. Build flexibility into program design to allow for incorporation of lessons learned into ongoing programming.

10. Identify and invest in change agents at all levels. At the local level, provide change agents with the tools and skills (such as leadership training) to support success.

The panel also discussed relationships between outside governments and host-country governments. The term "stabilization" is a foreign idea in many beneficiaries' eyes, although the government of Colombia implements stabilization activities. For any stabilization activity to succeed, it must be relevant to local context and presented through local nomenclature. Populations in countries emerging from conflict usually "do not ask for security, democratic security, or rehabilitation" but instead request immediate and simple services such as food, jobs, and shelter. The panel provided the following lessons learned for the Colombia context:

- Understand the local context: Adapt instruments to those needs.
- Respond: Provide massive, large-scale implementation and build large-scale organizational capacity.
- Spark and promote innovation: Pilot approaches and provide evidence for replication of innovations. Address legitimate, dominant, common local issues with scalable solutions.

LIBERIA LESSONS LEARNED

In Liberia, it was important to understand that security and development are linked and should be done in partnership. Liberia was able to transition the military from international to local ownership because of these partnerships by using locally relevant mechanisms for performing background checks on candidates for the police, in the absence of public records. Building partnership capacity is a "gateway capacity" that leads from security to development. Lessons include:

- Focus on all relevant elements (e.g., economic growth and security) simultaneously, rather than as a linear step-by-step process.

- Simplify. Try to make complex situations less complex, and remove obstacles. In Liberia's case that meant removing Charles Taylor from the country. Once he was gone, the warring armies agreed to a cease-fire and it stuck. Then West African peacekeepers could be brought in until the United Nations arrived.

- Internationalize the solutions. Create a multilevel web of peace to reduce backsliding and keep the peace process moving forward. The United States would have failed if it had attempted to do that unilaterally.

- Ensure the international mandate is appropriate to local context.

- Build legitimacy by working within the law and within relevant peace agreements. When Taylor left Liberia, the vice president was put in power in accordance with the law and peace agreements. Because of this, legitimate elections took place and today the president is perceived as the legitimate leader.

- Keep momentum on your side. Even when it may be tactically difficult, it is strategically critical that processes, such as disarmament of combatants, move forward.

- Finance your strategy. Without resources, there is no strategy.

- Create jobs and address rule of law and corruption.

- Place staff on the ground to quickly create an appropriate strategy and implementation plan; then let them implement it without undue interference.

The panel discussed the benefits and pitfalls of the privatization of security. Private companies are not beholden to U.S. government entities, so they are not encumbered by the institutional perspectives and biases of large bureaucratic institutions that can often inhibit innovation. They are also more efficient and flexible in hiring short-term technical assistance. On the other hand, a company that is motivated by profit could prolong the duration of a contract by providing information selectively. In addition, privatization of security could lead to a market for creating armies in foreign countries, or it could promote a culture of warlords becoming "Warlords, Inc." All institutions must rise together. For example, during the transition programs the Ministry of Finance was not able to pay the soldiers at the end of their training because the defense sector was ahead of the finance sector. It would have been appropriate in this instance to determine the size of the army not by the size of the outside threat but by the number of soldiers the country could reliably pay.

Working with Donors: A Conversation with Recipient-Country Officials

- **William Deng Deng**, Chair, South Sudan National DDR Commission

- **Rubén Zamora**, Ambassador of El Salvador to the United States

- **Husain Haqqani**, Ambassador of Pakistan to the United States (2008–2011)
- Moderator: **James Kunder,** Senior Resident Fellow, German Marshall Fund of the United States

The panel provided the following recommendations for working with donors on stabilization efforts.

- Partnerships are important. The development communities in recipient countries often will respond to donors, regardless of the relevance or appropriateness of a project design, because they need the money.
- Ownership needs to be built into the design of projects.
- Working with "proven" organizations that have been vetted and have performed well in the past is not always the most effective approach, because these organizations often do the work the donor wants, which may not reflect the needs of the country.
- Most successful projects include a senior adviser from the country. Project directors should be host-country nationals.
- Don't be a servant to the "cult of indicators" or let indicators dictate the course of the project. Flexibility and multilateral movement is needed.
- Be modest in setting your goals and desired outcomes.
- Consultants and NGOs should know the local context and have the right technical expertise. It is important that experts recognize the importance of implementing programs and projects differently from country to country. A successful model in one country may not work in another.

The panel addressed the importance of listening more to recipients, recognizing the importance of local culture and local context, and understanding the importance of honest dialogue. The panelists said that developing countries, such as Pakistan, are often looking for resources and already have innovative ideas. In addition, panelists said the United States often refers to developing country governments as "allies" but then runs the allies down with criticism and allegations of corruption and fraud. Cooperating country professionals do not perceive this as true partnership.

Overcoming the Operational Challenges to Donor Coordination

- **François Grignon**, Team Leader, Sudan/South Sudan, United Nations Department of Peacekeeping Operations (UN DPKO)
- **Jason Matus**, Senior Sudan Coordinator, AECOM

- **Jonathan Temin**, Director, Horn of Africa Program, Centers of Innovation, U.S. Institute of Peace (USIP)
- Moderator: **Andrew Natsios**, Executive Professor, Bush School of Government and Public Service

The panel discussed the need to address issues that led to the South Sudan crisis at the same time that the existing North-South crisis needs to be addressed. The shutdown of oil production in South Sudan deprived the country of 98 percent of its revenue. The government has since been operating from a need to protect itself. Therefore, any development strategy for South Sudan must factor in bilateral relations with Sudan, including addressing the Three Areas (Abyei, South Kordofan, and Blue Nile). We must find issues of commonality, such as water resources, and provide a forum to support economic development, governance, conflict mitigation, and other cross-border development issues. Armed youth also can be seen as potential opportunities for engagement rather than sources of conflict.

The fact that there was a joint agreement to divide the country and not a declaration of independence from South Sudan is another opportunity the development community can leverage to strengthen democratic institutions. The agreement addressed stability rather than development and governance. This was necessary because the country was on the brink of war. The development community must stop comparing South Sudan to Sudan and hold South Sudan to its self-declared standards, or to international standards. During this transition, it is important that the development community balance the transition from relief to development. It is time for the government of South Sudan to move to the forefront of its own development.

It is an ongoing problem that organizations are unable to engage with two of the most influential forces in South Sudan—the churches and the military—because of legal and ideological conflicts. The panel also addressed the relatively short tenure of USAID staff and military personnel in states like South Sudan, Afghanistan, and Pakistan where strong personal relationships are essential to building trust and affecting change; the usual one-year limit for personnel in hardship posts is insufficient.

Observations about the State of the Field

- **Robert Jenkins**, Acting Deputy Assistant Administrator, USAID Bureau for Democracy, Conflict, and Humanitarian Assistance (DCHA) and Executive Director of the Syria Task Force
- **Robert D. Lamb**, Director, CSIS Program on Crisis, Conflict, and Cooperation

Panelists recognized that while "international development" is now a mainstream academic discipline, industry goals and objectives must evolve to keep pace with a rapidly changing world. Aiming for stabilization is aiming too low. We must become more efficient at defining problems and setting relevant goals and objectives. It is difficult to measure what we are unable to define, so research and data collection are essential to justifying the need for any stabilization efforts.

The panelists reiterated the importance of respect for beneficiaries and host-country ownership of projects. The job of the international community is not to dictate solutions but to support communities to deliver the outcomes they have identified themselves. Over the past 10 years, the U.S. government has become more efficient, which has allowed USAID and NGO efforts to be more efficient and effective. This field has become much better at assessing changes as they flow through all the actors in a society, down to the community level. The development industry works within constrained budgets. In order to meet outcomes and be more effective, USAID and implementers must take more risks, and there must be an understanding that methods and strategies that worked in some countries may not be as effective in others.

Keynote Address: The Future of Stabilization

- **Frederick "Rick" Barton**, Assistant Secretary for Conflict and Stabilization Operations, U.S. Department of State

The remarks reviewed the need for the international community to recognize and respond to the changing face of conflict and crisis. A focus on "a fresh topic," which includes less Afghanistan and more "popular revolts," is needed. People in this field must address the changing face of conflict and conflict resolution to continue making impacts around the world. We need to shorten the calendar for the promised signs of progress—even if we accept the 20- or 40-year timeline. We need to create a "center of gravity" within the U.S. government that can react and make decisions quickly, rather than serving as a coordinator and convener. This decision authority does not have to reside in any one office, but in the best-suited office for the particular situation.

We also need to reshape our analytical lens, to be more inclusive. We should reach out to the silent majorities who dislike both the ruling elites and the opposition. We must expand views on local ownership, and hold host-country nationals accountable. This can be achieved by pressing local people to identify and address the needs and factors that are most important to them. The development community tends to build its own capacities, and not necessarily local capacity, even though increased local capacity and ownership offer the best chance for success. We have an important and catalytic role to play, especially during the first 18 months of any stabilization initiative. We should focus on the top few problems, as identified by local communities. It is essential to accept the enormity of the challenges and be persistent, and we should be opportunistic about who our partners are and what tasks we give them.

About the Authors

Robert D. Lamb is a senior fellow and director of the Program on Crisis, Conflict, and Cooperation (C3) at CSIS and a nonresident research scholar at the Center for International and Security Studies at the University of Maryland. Dr. Lamb studies governance and development amid conflict, with an emphasis on hybrid political systems and complex crises. He has presented his work to policymakers and experts throughout the United States and in Afghanistan, Colombia, France, Germany, Greece, India, Korea, Pakistan, Romania, Russia, Sweden, and the United Kingdom. A former Defense Department strategist, he has developed tools to help policymakers pay more attention to local governance and informal systems in places that terrorist, criminal, and insurgent networks use as safe havens. As a doctoral candidate, he spent a year in Colombia developing new methods for studying gang governance, violence, and legitimacy in the stateless slums of Medellín. He earned a Ph.D. in policy studies from the University of Maryland School of Public Policy in a program combining security, economics, and ethics. He received a B.A. in interdisciplinary studies from Gettysburg College, spent half a year in Nicaragua with a microdevelopment project, then worked for nine years as an editor and journalist, winning a National Press Club award in 2001, before changing careers after 9/11.

Kathryn Mixon is program coordinator and research assistant with the CSIS Program on Crisis, Conflict, and Cooperation (C3), where she researches absorptive capacity, nonstate-controlled areas, resilience, political transitions, and private-sector development in fragile states. Before joining CSIS, she conducted research for the Council on Foreign Relations and the Senate Foreign Relations Committee under Senator Richard Lugar, where she focused on crises in Belarus, Russia, and the European Union. Ms. Mixon earned a B.A. from the George Washington University in international affairs with a concentration in conflict and security and a minor in religious studies.

Joy Aoun is an adjunct fellow with the CSIS Program on Crisis, Conflict, and Cooperation (C3). She advises the program on the Middle East and North Africa (MENA), with a focus on Lebanon, Syria, and the broader Levant, and has contributed to the program's research on conflict, stabilization, potential transitions, and multilateral responses to global issues. Ms. Aoun specializes in state-society relations and the effects of peace treaties on the cohesion or fragmentation of national identities in postwar societies. Her areas of expertise include power-sharing arrangements and disarmament, demobilization, reintegration, and reinsertion (DDRR) mechanisms. She is frequently consulted by governments, nongovernmental organizations, and the private sector on the implications of instability and conflict in the MENA region. Prior to joining CSIS, Ms. Aoun worked on peace operations at the Center for International Studies and Research in Montreal (CERIUM). Fluent in English, French, Arabic, and Italian, she received a B.A. in history and international relations from Saint Joseph University in Beirut, Lebanon, and an M.S. in political science from the University of Montreal.

www.ingramcontent.com/pod-product-compliance
Ingram Content Group UK Ltd.
Pitfield, Milton Keynes, MK11 3LW, UK
UKHW051418150926
475561UK00005B/230

9 781442 227798